THE NATIONAL GALLERY SCHOOLS OF PAINTING

British Paintings

THE NATIONAL GALLERY SCHOOLS OF PAINTING

British Paintings

DILLIAN GORDON

Former Assistant Keeper,
The National Gallery

The National Gallery, London

National Gallery Publications
The National Gallery
London

Colour reproductions by P. J. Graphics Ltd, London W3
Printed by Henry Stone & Son (Printers) Ltd, Banbury

Front cover: detail from *Mr. and Mrs. Andrews* by Gainsborough
Back cover: detail from *The Fighting Téméraire* by Turner

THE NATIONAL GALLERY SCHOOLS OF PAINTING

This series offers the general reader an illustrated guide to all the principal schools of painting represented in the Gallery. Each volume contains fifty colour plates with a commentary and short introduction by a member of the Gallery staff. The first seven volumes in the series are:

Dutch Paintings by Christopher Brown
French Paintings before 1800 by Michael Wilson
Spanish and later Italian Paintings by Michael Helston
Italian Paintings of the Sixteenth Century by Allan Braham
Early Netherlandish and German Paintings by Alistair Smith
French Paintings after 1800 by Michael Wilson
British Paintings by Dillian Gordon

The first six volumes were published in association with William Collins.

Further volumes completing the series will be published shortly

Dr. Gordon was Assistant Keeper responsible for Earlier Italian and British paintings. She is the author of several books including *100 Great Paintings: From Duccio to Picasso*.

Introduction

The Collection of British pictures at the National Gallery is intended to show the best of British painting in the context of the European Collection, from the 18th to the 20th century. It includes major works by Hogarth, Gainsborough, Reynolds, Turner and Constable. The main body of the national collection of British paintings, together with European paintings from 1900, is housed in the Tate Gallery which was founded in 1897 by Sir Henry Tate and was at first administered by the National Gallery. Sir Henry presented his own collection of British pictures and to it were added some from Trafalgar Square. In 1954 the Tate Gallery was made independent and some more of the British and modern works from the National Gallery were transferred there. Transferal of paintings between the two galleries has continued to occur. The most recent was the return to the National Gallery of four paintings, – by Hogarth (see p.9), Gainsborough (see p.25), Wright of Derby (see p.45) and Sargent (see p.101) to mark the refurbishment of the Barry Dome and to bring the Collection more up-to-date by representing the 20th century.

The paintings described in this volume entered the Collection as gifts, bequests or purchases. The series called "Marriage à la Mode" by Hogarth (see p.9ff) was amongst the Angerstein Collection which formed the nucleus of the National Gallery in 1824. *The Cornfield* (see p.85) by Constable, for example, was presented as a tribute to the artist after his death. Some works by Constable were donated by his family. Turner bequeathed a large number of his works to the Nation in 1856, stipulating that some of them (see p.75 and p.77) were to hang alongside works by Claude Lorraine. A number of paintings came with the George Salting Bequest in 1910. The Gallery continues to pursue an active purchasing policy, the most recent acquisition being the double-portrait of *Mr. and Mrs. Coltman* (see p.49) by Wright of Derby which was purchased at auction in 1984.

PLATE 1

William Hogarth, 1697–1764

The Graham Children

Canvas, 160.5 × 181 cm.
Inscribed *W. Hogarth pinxt. 1742*
Presented to the National Gallery by Lord Duveen in 1934.
Transferred to the Tate Gallery 1952. Returned to the National Gallery 1986.

Hogarth was amongst the first British-born painters to establish a British "school" of painting. Before the 18th century, the leading artists working in Britain were largely foreigners: Rubens, Van Dyck, Lely, Kneller. One of Hogarth's early portraits was signed *W. Hogarth Anglus*, emphasising his own British-ness. He began by painting mostly conversation pieces and moralising subjects, but took up portrait painting in earnest in the late 1730s.

The portrait of the children of Daniel Graham, Apothecary to the Chelsea Hospital, who was appointed in 1739, was Hogarth's first successful large-scale group portrait. This major commission from Hogarth is an indication of the apothecary's prosperity.

The smallest child has a silver bowl brimming with fruit beside it, but perversely prefers the two cherries which the elder sister dangles tantalisingly out of reach. The other sister is mischievously engaged in dropping a mocking curtsey, while the boy turns a bird organ or "serinette" with a picture of Orpheus charming the beasts painted on its side.

It was perhaps to flatter the patron that Hogarth may have based this on Van Dyck's portrait of the Stuart children (Royal Collection, Windsor), but it is infinitely more "bourgeois". This painting of the charm and innocence of childhood also owes much to large-scale Dutch family portraits, not only in composition, but also in its use of emblems. The objects included may refer to the five senses: the fruits may represent taste, the organ hearing, the carnation smell, the painting sight, and the toy touch.

In the background, standing on a clock, a small golden cupid holds the kind of scythe used by Father Time, which reminds us that even childhood, however carefree and playful, is eventually cut down by Time. The life of the senses is mortal. Art and poetry are transient. The message is reinforced by the cat, ready to pounce on the bird the moment it tastes freedom from its cage. Despite its pessimistic symbolism, the freshness of colouring and charm of characterisation make it one of the loveliest and liveliest of Hogarth's paintings.

Richard Robert Graham, the boy turning the organ, who succeeded his father, still owned the painting in 1805. It may have passed out of the family at his death in 1816.

PLATE 2

William Hogarth, 1697–1764

Marriage à la Mode

Series of six. Each one canvas, 70 × 91 cm.
Transferred from the Tate Gallery, 1850.

The Marriage Contract

Hogarth introduced what he called a "novel mode"
of painting, namely the "painting and engraving of
modern moral subjects". His social satires were
didactic in their purpose. Many of his paintings were
intended for a wide public consumption through
prints. This is certainly true of the series *Marriage à
la Mode* in which all the compositions "read" from
left to right and which therefore made more com-
positional sense when reversed in an engraving. The
series, painted 1743–1745, was engraved in 1745. It
satirises the current practice of marriages between
the children of the wealthy middle classes and the
impoverished nobility.

In this picture the Marriage Contract is being
drawn up. The richly dressed but impoverished earl,
Lord Squander, has gout from dissolute living. Presented with his mortgage, he indignantly points to
his family tree. Resembling a tree of Jesse, it shows
that he is descended from William the Conqueror.
His coronet adorns pictures and furniture alike, and
even his footstool.

At the window his architect is admiring the plans
of his new mansion, still unfinished. While the mer-
chant scrutinises the contract, his miserable daughter
sits toying with her wedding ring, while the lawyer,
Counsellor Silvertongue, suggestively sharpening
his quill, woos her in whispers; her fiancé, a foolish,
fashionable dandy turns his back on her to admire his
own reflection as he takes snuff. On the wall the Old
Master paintings depict scenes of horror and grisly
martyrdom, portents of what is to come. And the
plight of the young couple is symbolised by the two
pathetic dogs, drooping and chained together.

PLATE 3

William Hogarth, 1697–1764

Shortly after the Marriage

Canvas, 70 × 91 cm.
Transferred from the Tate Gallery, 1850.

Late in the morning, after a night of debauchery, the
household of the newly-weds is in disarray. Smugly
provocative, the wife who has been breakfasting
alone, admires *her* reflection, while it is the husband's
turn to look dejected. Slumped in a chair, he is weary
after his night of whoring and brawling; his sword is
symbolically broken, and the dog is sniffing out a
woman's bonnet in his pocket. A yawning footman,
slovenly in his hair curlers, sleepily tidies up the
overturned chairs and spilled packs of cards, left after
a night of whist, music and love. Above the fireplace
an innocent cherub stoutly plays a tune called "O
Happy Groves"; in the other room a curtain over a
painting suggestively reveals – a foot. The steward
leaves with a sheaf of unpaid bills. He has in his
pocket a book of sermons entitled *Regeneration*. But
only degeneration lies ahead for the hapless young
couple.

PLATE 4

William Hogarth, 1697–1764

The Visit to the Quack Doctor

Canvas, 70 × 91 cm.
Transferred from the Tate Gallery, 1850.

The Viscount has brought his tearful young child-mistress, who has contracted venereal disease, to the quack doctor. Her bonnet seems to be the one sniffed out of the Viscount's pocket in the previous scene, and her blue cape and flowered skirt reflect the colouring of the Viscount's costume in the first scene. He seems to be complaining about the pills she has been given, of which a box lies between his legs on the chair. The leering doctor polishes his spectacles, while his virago companion prepares a knife, perhaps to operate on the girl (?). The objects in the room allude to sexual pleasure and the ghastly torments which may follow licentiousness: the horn of a unicorn hangs on the cupboard; within the cupboard a skeleton molests an *écorché*. The skull on the table as well as being there for medical purposes, suggests a *memento mori* and alludes to the future death of the Viscount.

PLATE 5

William Hogarth 1697–1764

The Countess's Morning Levée

Canvas, 70 × 91 cm.
Transferred from the Tate Gallery, 1850.

The Earl's coronets on the bed and mirror show that the old earl has died and the young couple have inherited the title. The Countess is now also a mother since a child's coral hangs from her chair. On the sofa is a licentious novel called *Le Sopha* and, putting his feet up, the lawyer Silvertongue, is making an assignation with the Countess offering her tickets for a masked ball. The masquerade on the painted screen prominently depicts a couple dressed as a friar and a nun. In the corner a small grinning negro joyfully unpacks the motley selection of objects which, as the catalogue on the floor shows, have just been bought from the sale of the collection of Sir Timothy Babyhouse including Lot 1000, the horned figure of Actaeon, alluding to the prospective cuckolding of the count. On the walls are the *Rape of Io* and *Rape of Ganymede* and *Lot's Daughters making their father drink wine*. Also hanging on the wall seems to be a portrait of Silvertongue himself.

While an Italian castrato, a fashionable singer of the time, and a flautist perform, their audience swoons, snoozes or affects to listen with rapt attention.

Cards on the floor include an indication of the Countess' social activities, such as card playing on a Sunday, and a misspelt enquiry: "Count Basset beg to no how Lade Squander Sleapt last Nite", as well as an invitation to Miss Hairbrain's.

As always in Hogarth, every object is a gloss on the situation.

PLATE 6

William Hogarth 1697–1764

The Killing of the Earl

Canvas, 70 × 91 cm.
Transferred from the Tate Gallery, 1850.

The scene takes place at a bagnio, as the paper on the floor near the fireplace shows. The Countess and her lover have had their assignation at the masquerade, dressed as the friar and nun shown in the screen in the previous scene. Their costumes lie discarded on the floor together with their masks. They have been surprised by the Earl who is shown dying from a wound inflicted in a duel by Silvertongue. The lawyer's bloody sword lies on the floor, while he escapes through the window. The Countess kneels, pleading for forgiveness. The master of the house and two members of the watch stand horrified in the doorway.

It has been pointed out that Hogarth based the poses of the Earl and Countess on the composition of *Noli me tangere*, underlining the theme of adultery in alluding to Mary Magdalene. Like Italian 17th-century painters, Hogarth is using the night scene to study the effects of different sources of light: the guttering candle and flames from the fireside catch the silver brocade and shoe buckles of the Earl and his glittering falling sword. The watch's lantern throws pools of light on the ceiling.

PLATE 7

William Hogarth 1697–1764

The Suicide of the Countess

Canvas, 70 × 91 cm.
Transferred from the Tate Gallery, 1850.

The last scene takes place at the house of the alderman the Countess's father: the arms of the City of London are on the windowpane. The view outside the window is of Old London Bridge; the houses on it were pulled down in 1756. Silvertongue has been caught and hanged for murder; his dying speech is reported in the broadsheet lying on the floor. At the news the Countess, who is not wearing mourning for the Earl, has taken poison and the bottle, marked *laudanum*, lies on the floor. The idiot servant is being scolded by an apothecary for fetching it for her. The Countess's diseased and crippled child who wears a plaster on its neck and an artificial leg, kisses its mother for the last time. The miserly alderman, wearing the same clothes as in the first scene, is removing the ring from his daughter's finger since at that time suicides forfeited their property. The ring is presumably the one she was first shown toying with so miserably. The lunch laid out on the filthy table cloth is being devoured by the starving skeletal dog. In the background the doctor is leaving, for he can do no more.

Hogarth began a series called *The Happy Marriage*, but it may be significant that he never finished it.

Hogarth treated the tragic downfall of his characters. He saw himself as a dramatic writer and his work was by its nature closely allied with literature. Consciously echoing Shakespeare, he wrote: "my picture is my stage, and men and women my players, who by means of certain actions and gestures, are to exhibit a *dumb show*."

PLATE 8

William Hogarth 1697–1764

The Shrimp Girl

Canvas, 63.5 × 52.5 cm.
Purchased, 1884.

Hogarth's lively sketch of a shrimp girl crying her wares, painted in about 1745, is unfinished. It is not known for what large composition, if any, Hogarth intended it.

In 1781 it was described as "a most spirited sketch in oil of a young fishwoman" and as being in the possession of Mrs. Hogarth. She kept it until she died in 1790. It may be that she modelled for it and that this explains her affection for and attachment to the picture. She used to tell visitors: "They say he could not paint flesh. There's flesh and blood for you".

PLATE 9

Thomas Gainsborough 1727–1788

Cornard Wood

Canvas, 122 × 155 cm.
Purchased, 1875.

Gainsborough was born in Sudbury, Suffolk and according to the artist himself this is one of his earliest landscapes. He said that it was painted in 1748 and represents a forest near Sudbury. Careful in its brushwork and organised composition, it is painted in the manner of the work of the 17th-century Dutch painter, Jacob Ruisdael. In his early years Gainsborough was greatly influenced by 17th-century Dutch painters. He is known to have restored a Wijnants and to have added figures to a Wijnants landscape.

In the last year of his life Gainsborough apologised for "Cornard Wood" as being "in some respects a little in the schoolboy stile". From boyhood until death, his love of landscape painting remained his abiding passion. When he was nearing death he spoke with touching nostalgia: " 'tis odd how all the Childish passions hang about me in sickness, I feel such a fondness for my first imitations of Little Dutch landskips that I can't keep from working an hour or two of a Day . . . I am so childish that I could make a kite, catch gold finches or build little ships".

PLATE 10

Thomas Gainsborough 1727–1788

Mr. and Mrs. Andrews

Canvas, 69.8 × 119.4 cm.

Purchased with a special Grant, and donations from the Pilgrim Trust, National Art Collections Fund, Mr. and Mrs. W. W. Spooner and Associated Television Limited, 1960.

After an apprenticeship in London with the engraver, Gravelot, Gainsborough set up as a portrait painter in his native town of Sudbury, Suffolk, in about 1748. In that year Robert Andrews (1726(?)–1806) married Frances Mary Carter (*c*.1723–80). This double portrait was probably painted a few years later, in about 1750. It shows Mr. Andrews having just returned from hunting, dishevelled, casually leaning on the back of the seat; prim Mrs. Andrews holds with distaste the pheasant he has just shot and which the dog wishes had been given to *him*. This area in Mrs. Andrews lap is unfinished: it may be that in the event Gainsborough shrank from a detailed depiction of a dead bird in the lap of so dainty a lady. The Andrews' farm, the Auberies, which was near Sudbury, is shown to be up-to-date in its lay-out: the planting of corn in rows, neat stacking of the sheaves, and enclosure of fields were all recent agricultural innovations. Unlike most of Gainsborough's landscape settings, the view is here identifiable; in the background is the church tower of St. Peter's Sudbury.

All his life Gainsborough had an exceptional feel for the effects of drapery, here evident in the rumpled beige jacket of Mr. Andrews, and the smooth sheen of his wife's blue dress. Drapery was to become for him one of the primary features of portrait painting.

PLATE 11

Thomas Gainsborough 1727–1788

John Plampin

Canvas, 50 × 60.5 cm.
Bequeathed by Percy Moore Turner, 1951.

Gainsborough had set up as a portrait painter in his native town of Sudbury, Suffolk in about 1748. He then moved to Ipswich in 1752. This portrait probably dates from the early 1750s. The sitter may be identifiable with John, son of John Plampin of Shimpling and Chadacre Hall (near Lavenham in Suffolk), who was born in 1727 and died in 1805. He inherited the Shimpling and Chadacre properties in 1757.

In Ipswich Gainsborough was visited by his friend, Philip Thicknesse, who was ecstatic about his landscapes, although he found his portraits "perfectly like, but stiffly painted, and worse-coloured". This portrait is typical of Gainsborough's Suffolk period portraits, which tend to be small-scale with stiff doll-like figures. Part of the awkwardness of Plampin's pose may be due to the fact that Gainsborough based it, reversed, on an engraving by Watteau of a certain Antoine de la Roque who had lost a leg at Malplaquet. Gainsborough much admired Watteau as "a very Fine painter taking away the French conceit", and his early work is influenced by French Rococo as well as 17th-century Dutch painting.

PLATE 12

Thomas Gainsborough 1727–1788

The Painter's Daughters Chasing a Butterfly

Canvas, 113.5 × 105 cm.
Henry Vaughan Bequest, 1900.

Gainsborough's married life was not one of unclouded domestic bliss. But he adored his two daughters, Mary, the elder, and her sister, Margaret, whom he painted several times during his life. This unfinished double-portrait dates from about 1756, the end of Gainsborough's Ipswich period, before he moved to Bath in 1759.

The youngest girl tries to catch a cabbage white (?) with her tiny hand, while just as optimistically, the elder hopes to throw her apron over it. The butterfly may symbolise the fragile transience of childhood, although in Italian Renaissance painting the butterfly symbolised the Resurrection and therefore hope. It is possible that Gainsborough had seen Hogarth's portrait of *The MacKinnon Children* of *c.*1742 (National Gallery of Ireland, Dublin) where a boy reaches for a butterfly poised on a sunflower.

Hand in hand, the two sisters represent one of the most enchanting images of childhood innocence ever painted. In sentiment the painting perhaps preludes Gainsborough's "fancy pictures".

Towards the end of Gainsborough's Suffolk period his handling loosens. The tight neat lines which he learned with Gravelot and Hayman, have given way to loose fluent brushstrokes, perhaps by virtue of studying Van Dyck in English country houses. This broader handling was also the result of this being one of his first nearly life-size portraits.

PLATE 13

Thomas Gainsborough 1727–1788

The Painter's Daughters Teasing a Cat

Canvas, 75.5 × 62.5 cm.
Purchased, 1923.

This double portrait was painted a year or two later than *The Painter's Daughters Chasing a Butterfly* (see p.31) and is also unfinished. The two little girls were apparently merciless in their tormenting of Nature. Here Mary, ostensibly hugging her younger sister, is actually tweaking the tail of the cat Margaret holds in her arms. Later portraits of the two sisters show them engaged in more sedate pursuits, such as sketching.

In both these early portraits of his daughters, Gainsborough was experimenting with a canvas prepared with a dark ground, on which highlights could very quickly be built up.

This picture remained for a long time in the family of Gainsborough's sister, Susanne.

PLATE 14

Sir Joshua Reynolds 1723–1792

Captain Robert Orme

Signed: *J Reynolds pinxit 1756*
Canvas, 240 × 147 cm.
Purchased, 1862.

Reynolds is supposed to have told his father he would "rather be an apothecary than an *ordinary* painter". In the event he was the first President of the Royal Academy in 1768 and the King's Principal Painter in 1784. After an apprenticeship with Hudson 1740–3, he visited Italy in 1749 and was able to make a first-hand study of the Antique and of Italian Renaissance artists, in particular Michelangelo and Raphael. His portrait of Captain Orme, painted in 1756, is based on a lunette fresco of the *Life of St. Francis* by the obscure Italian Renaissance painter, Iacopo Ligozzi, which Reynolds sketched in the cloister of the Ognissanti, Florence, in 1752. The fresco actually shows a standing soldier from the back, but Reynolds' sketch is so rough as to be ambiguous, and in reversing the composition, he perhaps misread it, and shows Captain Orme facing forward.

Robert Orme was a Lieutenant in the Coldstream Guards and aide-de-camp to General Braddock. He was wounded in an ambush by the French near Fort Duquesne, Pittsburgh, in 1755 and returned to England the same year. He resigned from the Army in 1756 when he became engaged to Audrey, daughter of the 3rd Viscount Townshend. Apparently Orme was unable to pay for the painting for Reynolds still owned it in 1761 when he exhibited it at the Society of Artists.

PLATE 15

Sir Joshua Reynolds 1723–1792

Anne, Countess of Albemarle

Canvas, 126.5 × 101 cm.

Purchased, 1890.

Lady Albemarle was the widow of the 2nd Earl of
Albemarle who died in 1754. She was the mother of
Admiral Keppel with whom Reynolds had sailed for
Italy in 1749 and whom he often painted. So he
knew his sitter well. She sat to him on a number of
occasions during the years 1757–9. This painting
appears to have been completed in 1760.

Lady Albemarle is shown engaged in the fashionable occupation of knotting. In her hands she holds a
knotting shuttle and the knotted thread wound into a
ball. Such knotted cord was used in fringes for
clothes and furnishings. On the table beside her is
her workbasket and a pair of scissors. Educated in the
Antique as he was, Reynolds would not have been
ignorant of the reference to the classical Fates cutting
the threads of life, a theme which may have been
suggested by her recent widowhood.

The paleness of her face may be attributable to the
type of carmine Reynolds used which has faded in
many of his portraits.

PLATE 16

Johann Zoffany 1733(?)–1810

Mrs. Oswald

Canvas, 226.5 × 159 cm.
Purchased, 1938.

Zoffany was born in Frankfurt am Main, Germany, and probably came to England in 1761. For a time he was probably employed as a drapery painter to Benjamin Wilson. He was a founder member of the Royal Academy. In 1772 he went to Florence at the expense of George III and spent some years there. He returned to England in 1779, but later travelled to India where he spent six years.

The sitter here is probably identifiable with Mary, daughter of Alexander Ramsay of Jamaica, who married Richard Oswald in 1750. She was widowed in 1784 and herself died in 1788. The couple lived on the estate of Auchincruive near Ayr.

Zoffany probably painted this portrait in the 1760's. Life-size portraits are unusual in his work. He normally painted small-scale conversation pieces, and theatrical scenes. Amongst his sitters was the famous actor, Garrick.

PLATE 17

Richard Wilson 1713/14–1782

Holt Bridge on the River Dee

Canvas, 148 × 193 cm.
Purchased, 1953.

Interest in landscape painting in England increased greatly during the 18th century. This was partly due to the fact that improved roads and travel conditions meant people could travel more easily and enjoy the countryside. During the 17th century, several Dutch and Flemish landscape painters had worked in Britain, or their work was collected by British connoisseurs, and visitors on the Grand Tour brought back, in particular, landscapes by Claude and Poussin. Admiration for these two painters was uncritical. A certain young lady corresponding from Italy during the 1790's wrote simply: "a Claude!!! a Claude!!!... a Claude!!!... a Claude!!!...Two landscapes by Claude!"

Although he finished his life in poverty, the Welsh painter, Richard Wilson, did what Gainsborough (see p.25ff.) would have loved to do, and became the first successful British landscape painter. He originally set up as a portrait painter, but in 1750 he went to Italy and it is there that he is supposed to have been urged by Zuccarelli in Venice and Vernet in Rome to become a landscape painter.

He began painting landscapes on commission in Italy, and on his return from Rome in about 1756 or 57, established a studio on the north side of the Great Piazza in Covent Garden.

The two companion landscapes of the Dee Valley (see p.43), probably painted in about 1762, seem to be real views adapted to suit the demands of a Claude-orientated public. The view of the Holt Bridge which joins Holt in Denbighshire to Farndon in Cheshire shows the tower of St. Chad's Church at Farndon on the right and the beginning of Holt on the left. The view is not topographically accurate, but has been arranged in accordance with the pastoral idylls of Claude, with figures idling in the foreground and the tree, cliffs, river and bridge organised in gentle diagonals to lead the eye back to the delicate light emanating from the horizon.

PLATE 18

Richard Wilson 1713/14–1782

The Valley of the Dee

Canvas, 148 × 193 cm.
Purchased, 1953.

The companion piece to *Holt Bridge on the River Dee* (see p.41), a view of the Dee Valley, may include the ancient town of Chester in the background. It also has something of the 17th-century Dutch painter, Cuyp, in the *contre-jour* effect of figures and animals on the brow of a hill, lit by the light flooding from the horizon.

The sense of space afforded by these birds' eye views is characteristic of much of Wilson's work. Wilson was a close friend of Joseph Wright of Derby (see p.45) and is supposed to have said: "With all my heart, Wright, – I'll give you *air*, and you'll give me fire".

It is not certain who commissioned the two paintings, although there is a possibility that it was Lionel, the 3rd Earl of Dysart who owned estates in Cheshire and had a seat at Woodhey, just east of Holt.

PLATE 19

Joseph Wright of Derby 1734–1797

Experiment with The Air Pump

Canvas, 182 × 243 cm.

Presented by E. Tyrrell to the National Gallery 1863.

Transferred to the Tate 1929. Returned to the National Gallery 1986.

Wright of Derby was one of England's most famous provincial portrait painters and for a brief period (1775–77) attempted to succeed Gainsborough in Bath. He also painted subject pieces and in 1772 was described as the "most famous painter now living for candlelights"; in his account book candlelight pictures were listed separately. Wright had a system of folding screens, so that his sitters could be in candlelight, while he himself sat in normal light. One of his most famous candlelit scenes, painted *c*.1767–8, shows an experiment with a device used for demonstrating the effect of a near-vacuum on animate and inanimate objects. Wright shows the dramatic moment when the air has been pumped out of the glass bowl and the dove is on the point of expiring, to the distress of the elder girl, who is being reassured, presumably, that at the reintroduction of air the bird will recover. On the left a man with a watch, perhaps Wright himself, times the exact moment when air is to be reintroduced to save the bird's life. The boy by the window is lowering the bird cage for the dove to be put back after the experiment.

The eeriness of the scene is accentuated by the fact that the actual light source is invisible, only reflected in the faces of the onlookers and in the fluid of a 'lung glass', while outside the window a full moon momentarily appears through the clouds. Wright seems to have included children in his painting as symbols of the future for whom the scientific discoveries of the dawning industrial age seemed then to promise so much.

PLATE 20

George Stubbs 1724–1806

The Milbanke and Melbourne Families

Canvas, 97.2 × 149.3 cm.

Purchased, 1975.

The sitters are from left to right: Elizabeth Milbanke, later first Viscountess Melbourne; her father, Sir Ralph Milbanke; her brother, John Milbanke, and her husband, Sir Peniston Lamb. Elizabeth Milbanke was only sixteen when she married in 1769. This portrait was painted a few months later when she was carrying her first son. It has been suggested that this is why she is shown in the very light type of carriage known as a "tin-whisky". The bright sparkle of Elizabeth Milbanke's dress and features, with the creamy whiteness of her shawl perfectly setting off the petal rose of her skirt, owes much to early Gainsborough – (see *Mr. and Mrs. Andrews*, p.27). She is the focal point of the painting and were it not for the fact that Stubbs used exactly the same tree in a contemporary portrait of *Colonel Pocklington with his wife and sisters*, one might attribute some symbolic significance to the way in which the trunk of the oak rises behind her to draw the rest of the figures within its shade. She became a formidable beauty, mistress of the Prince of Wales and mother of a Prime Minister.

PLATE 21

Joseph Wright of Derby 1734–1797

Mr. and Mrs. Coltman

Canvas, 127 × 101.6 cm.

Purchased with contributions from the National Heritage Memorial Fund and Pilgrim Trust, 1984.

This conversation piece, a double portrait of Mr. and Mrs. Thomas Coltman, was painted in 1770–71, perhaps to celebrate their recent marriage.

In 1769 Thomas Coltman (1746–1820) married Mary Barlow of Somerford Booths, Cheshire, who died in 1786. Following their marriage, the couple lived in Derby and apparently also at Gate Burton House, near Gainsborough, Lincolnshire; the façade here shown in the background closely resembles it. Wright painted a number of similar portraits on this scale, set in this type of landscape.

The couple are about to go riding: in the background a groom is bringing up a second horse. Coltman himself once wrote to a friend, Sir Joseph Banks: 'I propose to go out with the hounds in the morning which I can do more easily than write a letter'.

The Coltmans and Joseph Wright were close friends when they lived in Derbyshire, and the Coltmans owned a number of pictures by Wright including a *Self-Portrait* with a sketch for the *Air Pump* (see p.45) on the back.

The pose of Mr. Coltman is perhaps taken from Stubbs' *Milbanke and Melbourne Families* (see p.47) which was probably exhibited at the Society of Artists in 1770.

There is an interesting *pentimento* at the bottom of the tree trunk where Wright has painted out the horse's back right leg and changed its position.

PLATE 22

Thomas Gainsborough 1727–1788

Dr. Ralph Schomberg

Canvas, 223 × 153.5 cm.
Purchased, 1862.

In about 1760 Gainsborough moved from Suffolk to Bath and quickly secured for himself the monopoly of affluent and fashionable clientele. He was prolific in his output and of over 700 recorded portraits, about 150 are full-length. It took him normally just one month to complete two full-lengths. Although Gainsborough had a passion for landscape painting, business was, as he put it, "chiefly in the face way". However, he managed to set many of his portraits against a landscape background.

Dr. Ralph Schomberg (1714–94) was a Bath physician whom Gainsborough painted in about 1770, before Gainsborough moved to London in 1774.

Schomberg is posed casually, but elegantly, against a generalised rather turbulent landscape. Recent cleaning has revealed the very fine painting of his features. The pink of his coat is probably the result of an earlier working and has begun to show through with the fading of the brown.

PLATE 23

Sir Joshua Reynolds 1723–1792

Lady Cockburn and her three Eldest Sons

Signed: 1773/J REYNOLDS: PINX

Canvas, 141.5 × 113 cm.

Bequeathed by Alfred Beit, 1906.

Reynolds began this portrait on 1 September 1773 and it was completed by March 1774.

The children in the portrait were eventually to enter the Army, the Navy and the Church. The eldest child kneeling on the left became General Sir James Cockburn (1771–1852); the boy clutching his mother's neck became Admiral Sir George Cockburn (1772–1853) – he commanded *H.M.S. Northumberland* which conveyed Napoleon to St Helena; and the youngest child became the Rev. Sir William Cockburn (1773–1858). Their mother, second wife of Sir James Cockburn 8th Bart., was Augusta Anne who died in 1837 aged 88. The sitters were members of a now dormant baronetcy in the County of Berwick.

In showing the mother with her naked babies tumbling about her, Reynolds may have had classical representations of *Charity* in mind, perhaps one ascribed to Van Dyck and now in the Ashmolean Museum, Oxford, which was in Reynolds' own collection. The presence of the parrot is difficult to explain, except as a family pet.

Reynolds' placing of his signature and date in gold on the hem of Lady Cockburn's fur-lined robe may be an illusion to Raphael who sometimes inscribed his paintings of the Virgin and Child in this way.

PLATE 24

Thomas Gainsborough 1727–1788

The Watering-Place

Canvas, 147 × 180 cm.
Presented by Lord Farnborough, 1827.
Transferred from the Tate Gallery, 1953.

Gainsborough exhibited *The Watering-Place* at the Royal Academy in 1777. Its debt to Rubens was immediately recognised: Horace Walpole described it as "in the style of Rubens, and by far the finest landscape ever painted in England, and equal to the great masters". It may have been inspired by Rubens' version of the same theme, now also in the National Gallery, which excited Gainsborough's admiration in 1768 when it was in the collection of the Duke and Duchess of Montagu whose portrait he was then painting. The sweeping diagonals of the composition and way in which the light emanating from the horizon catches the trees, owes much to Rubens. The structure of the landscape, leading towards the hills in the background, is, however, fundamentally classical and derives from 17th-century French painting. Gainsborough remarked that "with respect to real views from Nature in this country" he had never seen "any place that affords a subject equal to the poorest imitations of Gaspar (Poussin) or Claude". In marked contrast to his emphasis on drawing from life in portraits, his landscapes were imaginary compositions. Although he made some drawings from Nature, he was famous for setting up model landscapes in his kitchen.

"He would place cork or coal for his foregrounds; make middle grounds of sand or clay, bushes of mosses and lichens, and set up distant woods of broccoli." He worked his imaginary compositions time and time again. The theme of cattle at a watering place frequently appears in very generalised sketches, with figures, trees, water, reeds and animals all treated with the same hatching process. While Gainsborough sought in his portraits to define those traits which marked out the sitter from his fellow beings, in his landscapes the figures blend with the countryside to create a tranquil and harmonious idyll. Gainsborough was never commissioned to paint a landscape. Landscape painting was his passion and remained his lifelong love, but brought no financial reward or recognition. When he died in 1788, *The Watering-Place* was still in his studio.

PLATE 25

Sir Joshua Reynolds 1723–1792

General Sir Banastre Tarleton

Canvas, 236 × 145 cm.
Bequeathed by Mrs. Henrietta Charlotte Tarleton, 1951.

During the American War of Independence, the sitter distinguished himself as a hero on the British side. He served under Lord Cornwallis in 1775 and returned to England as a Lieutenant-Colonel in about 1782. He became eventually M.P. for Liverpool and a General and a Baronet.

Reynolds began on this portrait in January 1782 and exhibited it at the Royal Academy in the same year. Gainsborough's portrait of the same sitter exhibited the same year is now lost. Reynolds shows him in the uniform of a troop raised during the American campaign known as the British Legion or Tarleton's Green Horse. In 1781 Tarleton lost two of the fingers of his right hand, as Reynolds shows.

PLATE 26

Thomas Gainsborough 1727–1788

Mrs. Siddons

Canvas, 126 × 99.5 cm.
Purchased, 1862.

Whereas Reynolds painted the actress, Mrs. Sarah
Siddons (1755–1831), as the *Tragic Muse*, Gainsborough painted his very formal portrait of her, completed by the end of March 1785, simply as a society
lady with no hint of the stage. Dignified in her stri-
ped satin dress, plumes, and furs, she fixes her gaze
away from the spectator. Her profile caused him
great difficulty as several *pentimenti* around the nose
show; he is supposed to have said, ambiguously,
"confound the nose, there's no end to it".

Gainsborough's portraits, in marked contrast to
his landscapes, were all painted from the life and
apparently with no preparatory drawings, which may
account for something of their immediacy. Although
he was always swearing "By St. Luke's pencil", and
although he made copious drawings of imaginary
landscapes, very few figure studies survive, which
suggests that he made few. He attached much
importance to a likeness, but his late portraits tend,
on the whole, to be devoid of great individuality. In
general he was perhaps more successful with female
rather than male portraits, because he could concen-
trate on the wonderful effects of silks, furs, ribbons
and the plumes of enormously elegant hats.

PLATE 27

Thomas Gainsborough 1727–1788

The Morning Walk

Canvas, 236 × 179 cm.

Purchased with a contribution from the NACF (Sir Robert Witt Fund), 1954.

The portrait was probably commissioned to commemorate the marriage between William Hallett and Elizabeth née Stephen which took place on 30 July 1785. Gainsborough received £126 for it on 4 March 1786.

It is one of the most beautiful of Gainsborough's late portraits. The transparent gauze of Mrs. Hallett's shawl and lace fichu, and the floating plumes of her hat with its pale green ribbon are rendered with light feathery brush strokes. He achieved this by standing equidistant from sitter and canvas and using six foot long brushes. The quick mercurial quality of the brushwork owes much to Van Dyck, whose portraits Gainsborough had so admired in English country houses, and of whom he said, "we are all going to heaven and van Dyck is of the party". Unlike other 18th-century portrait painters who employed studio assistants to complete the draperies, Gainsborough always painted the drapery himself. Although he attached much importance to what he called the "amazing effects of dress", these effects may be shimmering and elegant, but are never flamboyant. Here the colouring is subdued and gentle: the golden light, radiant in the background, catches the white silk of Mrs. Hallett's dress and lends warmth and a sense of the glowing freshness of dawn. The young couple, calmly together arm in arm, accompanied by a Spitz dog, were just embarking upon their married life; Gainsborough was nearing death. Poignantly he wrote in May 1788: "Hope is the pallat colours we all paint with in sickness". He died in August 1788. When Sir Joshua Reynolds paid tribute to him in his *Discourses*, he said of his great rival: "His regret at losing life was principally the regret of leaving his art."

PLATE 28

Thomas Gainsborough 1727–1788

The Market Cart

Canvas, 184 × 153 cm.

Presented to the National Gallery by the Governors of the British Institution 1830.
Transferred to the Tate in 1951. Returned to the National Gallery in 1986.

One of the most beautiful of Gainsborough's late landscapes, *The Market Cart*, was completed towards the end of 1786. The theme of peasants going to market with cartloads of produce was one often treated by Dutch and Flemish artists, such as Aelbert Cuyp and Rubens, both painters whom Gainsborough studied. The results are a blend of the Old Masters with natural observation. Gainsborough shows an autumn wood with the blue hills of a classical landscape in the background. The reds of the carrots and the girl's skirt, and the waistcoat of the woodgatherer, draw our attention, and create a link between the group in the cart and the woodgatherer, imparting a hint of narrative. Gainsborough's dreamy views of the English countryside, where Man and Nature blend into one harmonious and tranquil whole, were the expression of his own longings. He fretted constantly at "being confined in Harness to follow the track, whilst others ride in a wagon, under cover, stretching their Legs in the straw at Ease and gazing at Green Trees and Blue Skies".

PLATE 29

Sir Joshua Reynolds 1723–1792

Lord Heathfield, Governor of Gibraltar

Canvas, 142 × 113.5 cm.
Purchased with the rest of the Angerstein Collection, 1824.

Lord Heathfield, a distinguished soldier, was appointed Governor of Gibraltar in 1775, where he sustained a famous siege 1779–83. He is shown here with smoking cannon in the background, holding the key of Gibraltar in his hand and wearing the ribbon and star of the Order of the Bath. He sat for the painting in August and September 1787, but it was paid for by Alderman John Boydell who presented a copy of it to the Corporation of London in 1793. The painting has suffered much from the shrinking of the bituminous paint.

PLATE 30

George Stubbs 1724–1806

Lady and Gentleman in a Phaeton

Inscribed: '*Geo: Stubbs/pt. 1787*
Oak, 82.5 × 101.5 cm.
Presented by Miss H. S. Hope, 1920.

The sitters have not been positively identified, but it has been suggested that they may be members of the Hope family of bankers in Liverpool. The bluff genial gentleman and his comfortably buxom wife are unlikely to be members of the aristocracy, but rather of the wealthy middle class. Indeed they appear to be somewhat overwhelmed by their perhaps brand-new phaeton. The splendid horses, who proudly arch their necks, black against the subdued buffs of autumn, are without doubt the ones in control. It was Stubbs' analytical study of the *écorchés* and skeletons of horses (*The Anatomy of the Horse* was published in 1766) that enabled him to show the power of every muscle under their gleaming coats.

PLATE 31

Sir Thomas Lawrence 1769–1830

Queen Charlotte

Canvas, 239.5 × 147 cm.
Purchased, 1927.

This portrait, exhibited at the Academy in 1790, was one which helped to establish Lawrence's reputation as a painter. He was only 21 when he painted it and the Queen had found him "rather presuming". She herself chose the dress she wanted to wear, but Lawrence disliked her choice of bonnet, and she was shown bareheaded. She is wearing bracelets with a portrait miniature of George III and his cipher. In the background is a view of Eton.

Reynolds said to Lawrence: "In you, sir, the world will expect to see accomplished all that I have failed to achieve." Lawrence eventually succeeded Reynolds as Painter-in-Ordinary to the King in 1792, but the gleaming vivacity of his portraits owes perhaps more to Gainsborough than to Reynolds. In his portrait of Queen Charlotte he concentrated all his energies on the effects of the pale blue satin dress shot with lilac and the frothing of lace fichu and cuffs. For Lawrence had some difficulty with the Queen's features and even asked her to talk in order to lend them animation. Eventually she refused him further sittings and the Assistant Keeper of her Wardrobe, Mrs. Papendieck, modelled for the completion of the portrait.

PLATE 32

Sir Thomas Lawrence 1769–1830

John Julius Angerstein

Canvas, 91.5 × 71 cm.
Presented by William IV, 1836.

John Julius Angerstein was born in 1735 of a German family settled in Russia. He emigrated to England in about 1850 and was virtually the founder of Lloyds Bank in its modern form. His personal friends included Nelson, Johnson, Garrick, Sir Joshua Reynolds, and Sir Thomas Lawrence.

It was Angerstein's collection which formed the nucleus of the National Gallery in 1824. And it was a collection which was formed largely with the help of Lawrence. It consisted of important works by such painters as Raphael, Titian, Claude, Rubens and Hogarth, and was originally exhibited in Angerstein's town house, 100 Pall Mall, before the present building was built.

This portrait is an exact copy of an early portrait of Angerstein which Lawrence exhibited at the Academy of 1816. Lawrence painted it for George IV a few months after the sitter's death in 1823.

PLATE 33

Joseph Mallord William Turner 1775–1851

Calais Pier : An English Packet arriving

Canvas, 172 × 240 cm.
Turner Bequest, 1856.

Turner was born in Covent Garden, London, the son of a barber and wig-maker. He became a student at the Royal Academy in 1789 and exhibited his first oil painting there in 1796.

In 1802 Turner passed through Calais on his first journey abroad and in 1803 exhibited this painting at the Academy reflecting his own experiences of being "Nearly Swampt". In the subject-matter he was clearly influenced by Dutch marine and by shipwreck paintings. When exhibited, it was widely criticised as being unfinished in the foreground which was thought to have been painted with "blots".

PLATE 34

Joseph Mallord William Turner 1775–1851

Sun Rising through Vapour, Fishermen Cleaning and Selling Fish

Canvas, 134.5 × 179 cm.
Turner Bequest, 1856.

When Turner exhibited this painting at the Royal Academy in 1807, its reception was mixed. One critic thought it excellent; another wrote: "Turner has greatly fallen off in a large sea piece. He seems to have run wild with conceit". Although evidently deriving from Dutch seascapes, Turner's composition is very much his own. Although the pink reflection of the yellow sun, transformed in colour by the haze, is effective, it divides the picture and the whole is not as cohesive as in Turner's later works.

PLATE 35

Joseph Mallord William Turner 1775–1851

Dido Building Carthage, or The Rise of the Carthaginian Empire

Inscribed: DIDO BUILDING CARTHAGE OR THE RISE OF THE CARTHAGINIAN EMPIRE.
J M W Turner 1815
Canvas, 155.5 × 232 cm.
Turner Bequest, 1856.

The tomb on the right, inscribed "Sichaeo" is that of Dido's husband, whose murder by her brother originally led to her flight from Tyre to North Africa and the founding of Carthage.

Despite Turner's threats that he would be buried wrapped in this painting, Turner actually intended it to hang in the National Gallery, beside Claude's "Sea Port" and "Mill", and stipulated this in his bequest. For he admired Claude above all others. He is supposed to have burst into tears when he first saw a work by Claude and took every opportunity he could to study the French painter. Many of his works, such as this one, were painted in deliberate emulation of Claude. The classical buildings which dwarf the tiny figures, the "contre-jour" effect of the trees and the organisation of the composition all derive from Claude. And, as in Claude, the focal point of the dramatic narrative is not Dido herself, but the sun: symbolically rising over the horizon, it floods the scene with violently dazzling light, very different from the tranquil bobbing reflections of Claude's seascapes.

PLATE 36

John Constable 1776–1837

Weymouth Bay

Canvas, 53 × 75 cm.
Salting Bequest, 1910.

After seven years of courtship of Maria Bicknell, bitterly opposed by her family, Constable and Maria eventually married in St Martin-in-the-Fields on 2 October 1816. They spent their honeymoon with close friends, the Fishers, at their vicarage at Osmington. There Constable made a number of paintings and sketches of the Dorset coast, including this unfinished sketch of Weymouth Bay. The view looks to the west, taken from a little to the west of Redcliffe Point. The small Jordon River is seen flowing over the sands; Jordon Hill and Furzy Cliff are behind. Constable worked out of doors, achieving an effect of immediacy and spontaneity. However, he also studied the work of previous landscape painters and in this sketch the influence of 17th-century Dutch seascape painters is particularly in evidence in the expansive sweep of the bleak deserted coastline, and a large part of the composition given to the study of the sky, with the clouds puffing over the horizon. Constable considered the sky the "key note", the "organ of sentiment"; "[it is] the source of light in Nature and governs everthing".

PLATE 37

John Constable 1776–1837

Salisbury Cathedral and Archdeacon Fisher's House from the River

Canvas, 52.5 × 77 cm.
Salting Bequest, 1910.

Constable described his initial concept as "Church under a Cloud". He began painting Salisbury Cathedral during his visits to his dearest friend, Archdeacon John Fisher, who in 1819 was granted for life the use of the Canonical Hall, Leydenhall, shown here partly hidden by trees. In the foreground is the River Avon; on the left are the grounds of King's House, with the spire of the Cathedral behind.

This sketch probably dates from 1820, when Constable went to stay with Fisher for two months.

Constable's studies of Salisbury Cathedral culminated in his "Great Salisbury" – "Salisbury Cathedral from the Meadows" (Private Collection) which he exhibited at the Royal Academy in 1831.

PLATE 38

John Constable 1776–1837

The Hay Wain

Canvas, 130.5 × 185.5 cm.
Signed: *John Constable pinx'. London 1821*
Presented by Henry Vaughan, 1886.

When *The Hay Wain* was exhibited at the Royal Academy in 1821, it failed to please. Its bright fresh colours, thickly applied paint, and naturalness were anathema to a public which idolised the idealised landscapes of Claude, with their classical ruins and golden Italian light. Constable, however, by no means ignored the achievements of landscape painters of the past. His use of high view point and strong diagonals owe much to Rubens. He was also interested in investigating in detail the transient phenomena of the natural world, particularly the sky, with its changing effects of light and clouds (see p.79). The realism of his landscapes derives from the

direct observation of Nature and countless studies made out-of-doors. He particularly studied his native Suffolk. Here the view is of Willy Lott's cottage on the river Stour, painted from Flatford Mill, of which Constable's family had the tenancy. The scene is specific, as is the time of day. Although Constable himself referred to it as the "Wain", it was actually exhibited at the Royal Academy under the title "Landscape, Noon". Later Constable used exactly the same title for *The Cornfield* (see p.85) which he accompanied in the exhibition catalogue with a quotation from Thomson's *Summer*:

"A fresher gale
Begins to wave the woods and stir the stream
Sweeping with shadowy gusts the fields of corn."
And indeed the two paintings are very similar. The realism of "The Hay Wain" excited much admiration when it was exhibited in 1824 at the Paris Salon, where it was awarded a gold medal, and the remark was overheard: "Look at these English pictures – the very dew is on the ground". However, as the signature emphasises, the studies may have been out-of-doors, but the final version was completed back in his London studio. After making various sketches, Constable mapped out his ideas in a full-scale study (London, Victoria and Albert Museum). In the final version he made a few changes, omitting a figure on horseback at the edge of the stream and substituting a barrel, which he eventually painted out, and which is now beginning to show through. In 1821, a few months after he had completed this picture, he wrote to a friend: "But the sound of water escaping from Mill dams, . . . willows, old rotten banks, slimy posts, and brickwork. I love such things . . . As long as I do paint I shall never cease to paint such places".

PLATE 39

John Constable 1776–1837

The Cornfield

Signed: *John Constable f. London 1826*
Canvas, 143 × 122 cm.
Presented by a body of subscribers, 1837.

Three days after Constable's death in 1837, his friends gathered at his house and between them they chose a painting which would testify to his greatness: the painting was *The Cornfield* which was the first painting by Constable to enter a national collection. It was presented by a body of 105 subscribers which, under the Chairmanship of Sir William Beechey, included Faraday and Wordsworth. Constable's son identified the view as probably of a path leading from East Bergholt in Suffolk to Dedham, except that the church is an invention. It has been pointed out that this would have been the path he would have followed to school in Dedham during what he called his "careless boyhood" in Suffolk. When Constable described the picture to his friend, John Fisher, it was in terms of Thomson's poem *Summer*: "while now a fresher gale, *sweeping with shadowy gusts the fields of corn . . .*" (Constable's italics). It is significant that the tower of the church, which provides the central focal point of the composition should not be topographically accurate. For the organisation of the composition is very much along the lines of a French 17th-century classical landscape and particularly corresponds with Claude's *Hagar and the Angel* (National Gallery). This was a picture owned by Sir George Beaumont who took it everywhere with him. Constable's biographer, Leslie, said that he "looked back on the first sight of this exquisite work as an important epoch in his life".

Painting his memory of the scenes of his Suffolk boyhood in his studio in London with evident nostalgia, Constable has not forgotten Claude, whose work he so admired. He made two copies of another landscape by Claude in Sir George Beaumont's collection, also now in the National Gallery, which, significantly he described as "a noon day" scene, like *The Cornfield* and added: "It contains almost all that I wish to do in landscape".

PLATE 40

Joseph Mallord William Turner 1775–1851

Ulysses Deriding Polyphemus

Canvas, 132.5 × 203 cm.
Turner Bequest, 1856.

This painting was exhibited in 1829.

The subject comes from Book IX of the Odyssey.
Ulysses stands on his ship with his companions
deriding the Cyclops he has just blinded.

Ruskin called this "the *central picture* in Turner's
career", noting how closely Turner kept to Pope's
translation of the Greek text: the horses of the Sun
God rise above the horizon, and Ulysses' ship is
"in the shallows clear". It has been suggested that
Turner was using the picture to illustrate the forces
of nature and also that the heightened colour is the
result of the study of Early Renaissance paintings
Turner saw on his second visit to Italy in 1828. And
indeed, when Turner exhibited the painting it was
criticised for "*colouring run mad*".

PLATE 41

Joseph Mallord William Turner 1775–1851

The Evening Star

Canvas, 92.5 × 123 cm.
Turner Bequest, 1856.

Painted in about 1830, this is perhaps one of
Turner's most haunting and poetic images. A child
and frisking dog, leaving the sands after shrimping,
are wraith-like in the paleness of evening. The sun
has just sunk below the horizon, leaving a smattering
of pink clouds. The evening star, brightly extended
in its reflection in the gloomy sea, is a single dab of
paint in a plain and otherwise empty sky. The poles
of lobster pots and fishing nets are forlorn and iso-
lated.

PLATE 42

John Constable 1776–1837

The Cenotaph to Reynolds' Memory, Coleorton

Canvas, 132.1 × 108.6 cm.
Bequeathed by Miss Isabel Constable, as the gift of Maria Louisa, Isabel and Lionel Bicknell, 1888.

In 1823 Constable made a prolonged visit to the country seat of Sir George Beaumont, Coleorton Hall, Leicestershire. There he made a drawing of the Cenotaph to Sir Joshua Reynolds which stood in the grounds. On the back of the drawing he copied Wordsworth's inscription which had been commissioned to express Beaumont's feelings of "What England lost when Reynolds died". Ten years later, Constable made the drawing a basis for a painting of the monument, adding on either side the busts of Michelangelo and Raphael, the two artists whom Reynolds had admired above all others. He completed the painting in 1836. It was his last important work before he died in March 1837.

The painting is typical of Constable's late work which tends to be gloomy in palette, heavy with *impasto*, and densely painted.

PLATE 43

Joseph Mallord William Turner 1775–1851

The Parting of Hero and Leander

Canvas, 146 × 235 cm.
Turner Bequest, 1856.

The story of the two lovers, Hero and Leander, was told by the ancient Greek grammarian and poet, Musaeus. Leander, a youth of Abydos, used nightly to swim the Hellespont to join Hero, the priestess of Aphrodite at Sestos, guided by the lamp she placed at the top of a tower. One night the lamp went out and Leander died. Hero then flung herself into the sea. Turner's turbulent version of the story shows Leander being dragged under by spectres. In the background phantasmagoric architecture, building piled upon building, the frenzied figures in the foreground, and the unnatural reflections cast by the moon render the story nightmarish and fantastical.

Turner exhibited the painting at the Royal Academy in 1837.

PLATE 44

Joseph Mallord William Turner 1775–1851

The 'Fighting Téméraire' Tugged to her last Berth to be broken up 1838

Canvas, 91 × 122 cm.
Turner Bequest, 1856.

The 'Téméraire' took its name from a French ship captured at Lagos Bay in 1759. She was a warship of 98 guns launched at Chatham in 1798. Her crew under Captain Eliab Harvey distinguished themselves at the Battle of Trafalgar in 1805, after which she was known as 'The Fighting Téméraire'. In 1838 she was sold out of service and towed from Sheerness to Rotherhithe to be broken up. Turner shows the graceful yet lumbering hulk of the wooden ship with her delicate masts and rigging, being ignominiously towed by a squat spitting tug: sail was being replaced by steam. The rays of the setting sun painted in raw brilliant impasto are gloriously but sadly defiant, a mood echoed in the verses with which the painting was first exhibited by Turner:

"The flag which braved the battle and the breeze,
No longer owns her".

PLATE 45

Joseph Mallord William Turner 1775–1851

Rain, Steam and Speed – The Great Western Railway

Canvas, 91 × 122 cm.
Turner Bequest, 1856.

While Constable showed Nature undisturbed by the developments of the Industrial Revolution, Turner was all too aware of its imminent effect on daily life.

Two figures are peacefully boating on the Thames. Above them the train is crossing Maidenhead railway bridge, spanning the Thames between Taplow and Maidenhead. The bridge, which was begun on Brunel's design in 1837, was completed in 1839. Turner exhibited this painting at the Academy in 1844. Running in front of the train is the symbol of natural speed, a hare. But it is inevitable that the hare will be caught up and suffer the fate of Carker, who was mangled by an engine at the end of Dickens' *Dombey and Son* (1848). The black fiery engine is an aggressive intrusion into the "tinted steam" of the river landscape, where water and sky are an indeterminate mingling of light and reflection.

When the painting was exhibited, it caused general amazement and one critic wrote: "The world has never seen anything like this picture".

PLATE 46

Joseph Mallord William Turner 1775–1851

Margate from the Sea

Canvas, 90 × 120 cm.
Turner Bequest, 1856.

Painted between about 1835 and 1840, the subject of
this painting is so abstract as to be indeterminate.
Many of Turner's late paintings are simply studies of
the effects of light and water, thickly painted with
generous application of paint and smeared impasto.
The results are a dazzling brightness.

PLATE 47

John Singer Sargent, 1856–1925

Lord Ribblesdale

Inscribed: *John S. Sargent, 1902*

Canvas, 253 × 149 cms.

Presented in 1916 to the National Gallery by Lord Ribblesdale as a memorial to Lady Ribblesdale and his sons – Captain the Hon. Thomas Lister, D.S.O., 10th Hussars, killed at Jidballi, Somaliland; and Lieut. the Hon. Charles Lister (H.M. Diplomatic Service), Hood Battalion, R.N.D., who fell in Gallipoli, 1915. Transferred to the Tate Gallery 1926. Returned to the National Gallery in 1986.

Sargent, who was born in Italy of American parents, trained in Florence and Paris. He settled in London in 1884/5 and became the fashionable society painter of the Edwardian era. Amongst his sitters were Henry James, George Meredith, Gabriel Fauré, as well as members of the aristocracy, and it was he who drew Edward VII on his death bed. His free brilliant style expresses with verve and panache an age which was flashy and stylish to the point of vulgarity.

Thomas Lister, 4th Baron Ribblesdale (1854–1925) is here shown wearing hunting costume. He was Master of the Buckhounds from 1892 to 1895 and author of *The Queen's Hounds and Stag-Hunting Recollections*. He became a Trustee of the National Gallery in 1909.

Index to Plates

Note: page numbers throughout refer to the position of the illustrations